FLY GUY PRESENTS: WEIRD ANIMALS

Tedd Arnold

Scholastic Inc.

For Charlie and Sammy!

Photos ©: cover: Herman Menkz/Getty Images; back cover: Kerryn Parkinson/NORFANZ/Caters News/ZUMA Press; 4–5: Betty LaRue/Alamy Stock Photo; 6: Nicholas Smythe/Science Source; 7 left: Dorling Kindersley/Getty Images; 7 right: Globe Turner/Shutterstock; 8: Joel Sartore/Getty Images; 9 top: Heidi & Hans-Juergen Koch/Minden Pictures/Superstock, Inc.; 9 bottom: Raymond Mendez/Animals Animals/age fotostock; 10 top: Edwin Butter/Shutterstock; 10 center: Juniors Bildarchiv GmbH/Alamy Stock Photo; 10 bottom: Kim Harrington/500px/Getty Images; 11 top: Auscape/UIG/Shutterstock; 11 bottom: Sergey Gorshkov/Minden Pictures; 12: Brandon Cole Marine Photography/Alamy Stock Photo; 13 top: Stephen Frink Collection/Alamy Stock Photo; 13 bottom: BIOSPHOTO/Alamy Stock Photo; 14: Tsunemi Kubodera of the National Science Museum of Japan, HO/AP Images; 15 top: HO, National Science Museum/AP Images; 15 center left: BIOSPHOTO/Alamy Stock Photo; 15 center: fenkieandreas/Shutterstock; 15 center right: Genevieve Vallee/Alamy Stock Photo; 15 bottom: imageBROKER/Alamy Stock Photo; 16 top: Nature Picture Library/Alamy Stock Photo; 16 bottom: Paulo Oliveira/Alamy Stock Photo; 17 top: The Natural History Museum/Alamy Stock Photo; 17 bottom: CB2/ZOB/WENN.com/Newscom; 18: Kerryn Parkinson/NORFANZ/Caters News/ZUMA Press; 19 left: Kyodo News Stills/Getty Images; 19 right: Vallorie Francis/Alamy Stock Photo; 20 top left: Martin Pelanek/Dreamstime; 20 top right: Jason Edwards/Getty Images; 20 bottom: De Agostini/Getty Images; 21 top: Auscape International Pty Ltd/Alamy Stock Photo; 21 bottom: Hugh Lansdown/Shutterstock; 22 top: D. Parer & E. Parer-Cook/ardea.com/Mary Evans Picture Library Ltd./age fotostock; 22 bottom: Nature Picture Library/Alamy Stock Photo; 23 top: NHPA/Superstock, Inc.; 23 center: Biosphoto/Superstock, Inc.; 23 bottom: Avalon/Photoshot License/Alamy Stock Photo; 24 top: Susan Schmitz/Shutterstock; 24 bottom: Detlef Knapp/500px/Getty Images; 25 top: Muhammad Otib/EyeEm/Getty Images; 25 background: Joanna Stankiewicz-Witek/Shutterstock; 26: George D. Lepp/Getty Images; 27 top left: Irina Orlova/Shutterstock; 27 top right: Agency-Animal-Picture/Getty Images; 27 bottom: INTERFOTO/Alamy Stock Photo; 28 top: Dalibor Valek/Shutterstock; 28 center: Stephen Hutchison/500px/Getty Images; 28 bottom: Silvia Pascual/Shutterstock; 29 top: 548901005677/Getty Images; 29 center: Dorling Kindersley ltd/Alamy Stock Photo; 29 bottom: Andras Deak/Shutterstock; 30 top: Image by Luiz Rocha © 2017 California Academy of Sciences; 30 bottom: Zwiebackesser/Shutterstock; 31 top: Trustees of the Natural History Museum and Scientific Associate of the Museum, Dr. Michael Darby; 31 bottom: Franz Perc/Alamy Stock Photo.

Library of Congress Cataloging-in-Publication Data available

ISBN 978-1-338-68178-9

10 9 8 7 6 5 4 3 2 1   21 22 23 24 25

Printed in the U.S.A.   113
First printing, February 2021

Book design Marissa Asuncion

A boy had a pet fly named Fly Guy.
Fly Guy could say the boy's name —

Buzz said, "Being an animal would be
weird. Let's learn more about them."

Buzz and Fly Guy arrived at the science museum. They were there to see the weird animals exhibit.

I can't wait to see the cool creatures inside.

Let's go, Fly Guy!

Buzz and Fly Guy went up to the first display. The pink fairy armadillo is the smallest armadillo alive today. An adult is only 5 to 6 inches long. These tiny creatures have pink armor covering their furry bodies.

Only a few pink fairy armadillos have been spotted in the wild!

Pink fairy armadillos use their front claws to dig underground burrows. They sleep during the day and live alone. They live in the dry, sandy grasslands of central Argentina.

Naked mole rats live in underground burrows in eastern Africa.

They have wrinkly, mostly hairless bodies. They are nearly blind. Whiskers on their faces and tails help them feel their surroundings.

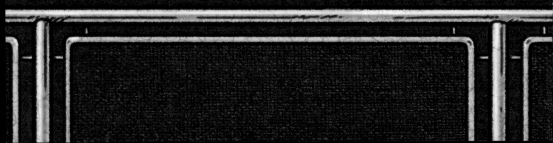

A naked mole rat colony has a queen and many workers. Worker rats dig new tunnels using their strong teeth. They can move their teeth separately, like chopsticks!

Naked mole rats can live for more than 30 years!

Making Burrows!

Prarie dogs live in underground burrows. They are found in the central and western grasslands of the United States.

Atlantic ghost crabs dig burrows in the sand. The burrows can be 4 feet deep. The crabs crawl underground to hide from the sun. They also hide from from predators like raccoons, shorebirds, and gulls.

Eastern chipmunks store food for winter in their burrows. They gather nuts and seeds. Then they hide them in an underground chamber. The chamber can be up to 10 feet long.

Monitor lizards (or goannas) in western Australia build corkscrew-shaped burrows. They can be 8 to 10 feet deep. The lizards lay their eggs in a chamber at the bottom. This keeps them safe until they hatch.

COZY!

Arctic foxes live in burrows that have up to 100 entrances. During a blizzard, both arctic foxes and polar bears will dig chambers into the snow. This keeps them warm and safe.

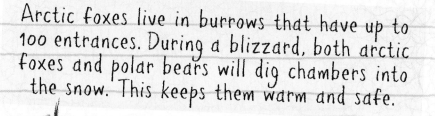

The ocean is full of weird animals, like the Portuguese Man o' War. This creature isn't a jellyfish. It isn't a single animal either. It is a siphonophore (sahy-fuh-nuh-fawr) —a group of identical clones that work together as one.

Each Portuguese Man o' War has a blue or purple bubble shaped like a sail. This bubble floats on top of the water. It is pushed along by the wind or ocean currents.

Underwater, 30- to 165-foot-long tentacles trail along. The tentacles catch small fish and crustaceans and sting them with poisonous venom. While a Portuguese Man o' War sting is painful to humans, it usually isn't deadly.

Man o' War? I'm all about peace and love, man!

The sea is home to another misunderstood creature, the giant squid. Very few have been seen in the wild. This is because they live deep down in the ocean. For years people thought these giants were the fictional kraken. Sailors believed this sea monster hunted and sank huge ships.

YIKEZ!

Giant squids have the largest eyes of any animal in the world. They're as big as basketballs!

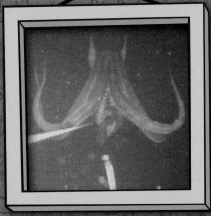

In real life, giant squid are not monsters. They are cephalopods (sef-uh-luh-pods). Squid, octopus, cuttlefish, and nautilus are all types of cephalopods.

CUTTLEFISH

OCTOPUS

SQUID

NAUTILUS

Giant squid live all over the world. They grow to be up to 43 feet long. Some scientists believe they may grow to be even bigger! Most weigh about 1,000 pounds.

Deep Ocean Discoveries

The Mariana Trench is the deepest place on Earth. This canyon is in the western Pacific Ocean. It is more than 1,500 miles long and 43 miles wide. The deepest point is almost 7 miles below the ocean's surface!

It is very dark in the Mariana Trench. The seadevil anglerfish uses a built-in headlight to lure prey.

Deep-sea hachetfish have bioluminescent bodies. These tiny, skinny fish can brighten or dim their glow to hide from predators.

Osedax worms (also called zombie worms) survive by eating fish bones and dead animals. They use special bacteria to turn the bones into food.

Amphipods are huge shrimp-like crustaceans. Those in the Mariana Trench can be more than a foot long! Scientists think small molecules in their cells help them survive the intense water pressure.

This deep, the water is pitch black and freezing cold. The pressure is crushing. The animals that live there have adapted in surprising ways.

The blobfish was discovered off the coasts of New Zealand and Australia in 2003. It was once voted the world's ugliest animal. This misunderstood creature lives at depths of 2,000 to 4,000 feet.

Each blobfish is about a foot long and weighs up to 20 pounds.

OCEAN SURFACE

OCEAN BOTTOM

CRUNCH

The blobfish has very soft bones, like a jellyfish. Its gelatinous body is only slightly denser than water. At sea level this makes the blobfish look droopy and weird. But down deep, this strange-looking fish is a survivor.

A blobfish can survive water pressure that would crush a submarine!

When it comes to odd animals, the duck-billed platypus tops the list. Like other mammals, the platypus is warm-blooded. It has a backbone, and feeds its young milk. But the platypus lays eggs like a reptile. It also has webbed feet and a bill like a bird—all unusual for a mammal.

What's more, male platypuses have poisonous stingers on their back feet.

These make them one of the world's few venomous mammals.

Platypuses live in rivers and wetlands in eastern Australia. They hunt underwater. They paddle with their webbed feet and steer with their big, beaver-like tails.

The echidna is the only other mammal in the world that lays eggs!

Venomous Mammals

Most mammals use their sharp claws and teeth to catch prey and defend themselves. But there are a few mammals that use venom, too!

A venomous stinger on a male platypus.

GROZZ!

SLURP

The slow loris may look cute, but this primate has a deadly bite. When threatened, the slow loris licks venomous glands under its arms. This gives its saliva a poisonous kick.

The North American short-tailed shrew uses its venomous saliva to paralyze insects and worms. It then stores them to eat later. A preserved mealworm can last for two weeks.

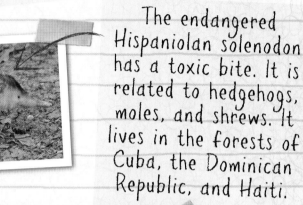

The endangered Hispaniolan solenodon has a toxic bite. It is related to hedgehogs, moles, and shrews. It lives in the forests of Cuba, the Dominican Republic, and Haiti.

Vampire bats use their sharp teeth to bite cows and drink their blood. Venom in the bat's saliva isn't deadly. It keeps the cow's blood from clotting so the bat can eat.

At 2 to 3 feet long, this creature may look like a miniature dragon. It is really a frilled lizard! It is one of the strangest sights in the forests of northern Australia and southern New Guinea. This reptile has a thin piece of skin around its neck called a frill.

The frill usually lies flat. If the lizard feels threatened, surprise! It opens its yellow mouth and unfolds the colorful fan of skin. This scares off predators.

Many animals can make themselves look bigger to be scary, but that is just plain weird!

Fleas are small, flightless insects. They survive by eating the blood of animals or people. There are more than 2,500 species of flea! The most common is the cat flea. The cat flea lives on dogs, cats, and humans. These tiny pests can also carry diseases, including bubonic plague.

ITCHEZZ!

What do you call a happy flea? A hop-timist!

Fleas are incredible jumpers. A single flea can leap more than 200 times its own length.

One flea can lay 50 eggs a day!

From the 1830s through the 1960s, flea circuses were popular in England and Germany. Miniature displays showed fleas "performing" by jumping through hoops. They also operated tiny machines, carriages, Ferris wheels, or carousels.

Roloff's Floh-Circus

Wacky & Weird Q&A

Even ordinary animals have unusual features . . .

Q: Which animal has sensors on its face that help it navigate in the dark?
A: A cat!

Q: Which animal's nose produces a special mucus that absorbs scents?
A: A dog!

Q: Which bird is the fastest swimmer?
A: A Gentoo penguin!

Q: Which animal dads give birth to their babies?
A: Seahorses, pipefish, and sea dragons!

Q: Which animal tastes with its body, wings, and feet?
A: **FLYZZZZZ!**

Q: Which animal has about 14,000 teeth in rows on its tongue?
A: A garden snail!

Q: Which animal has fingerprints that look just like a human's?
A: A koala!

The human species has caused many changes to Earth's ecology. It is more important than ever for scientists to study the many forms of life on our amazing planet.

There is still so much we don't know about the natural world. Every year, scientists describe and name hundreds of new plant and animal species!

The tiny, bright neon-colored coral fish *Tosanoides aphrodite* was named after Aphrodite. She is the Greek goddess of love and beauty.

The largest group of new species discovered in 2019 was beetles. One of these, *Nelloptodes gretae* was named after the Swedish climate activist Greta Thunberg.
NEW SPECIEZZZZ!
I will name it Buzzes Bugsey.

"I can't believe how many weird animals are all around me," said Buzz. "Including you, Fly Guy. You are really weird!"

Fly Guy and Buzz headed home. They were excited to plan their next adventure.